SCHIRMER'S LIBRARY OF MUSICAL CLASSICS

Vol. 1832

FRANZ SCHUBERT

Sonata
(Per Arpeggione)

For Viola and Piano

Viola part edited
and fingered by
PAUL DOKTOR

G. SCHIRMER, Inc.

DISTRIBUTED BY
HAL•LEONARD®
CORPORATION
7777 W. BLUEMOUND RD. P.O. BOX 13819 MILWAUKEE, WI 53213

Photograph of an Arpeggione

Preface

The "Arpeggione" was a guitar-like instrument tuned in the same way as the guitar (E A d g b e'), but held between the knees and played with a bow. Invented in 1821 by the Viennese guitar maker Johann Georg Stauffer (1778-1853), it was originally called "Guitarre d'amour," but soon dubbed "Arpeggione" because it lent itself so well to arpeggio playing. However, its peculiar guitar-like body made adequate performance on it very awkward; especially in loud passages it was very difficult to keep the bow on one string only. But the instrument possessed a warm sound quality, and it was this attribute which Schubert exploited in the sonata which he wrote for it in 1824. Naming his composition *Sonata for Arpeggione,* he honored the instrument's nickname by making it, so to speak, official. However, despite the attention brought to the new instrument through public performances of the Schubert work by Vinzenz Schuster, and the publication of an instruction book by the same musician, the arpeggione soon became obsolete: its beauty of tone could not make up for its playing difficulties and rather small volume of sound.

Schubert's manuscript in the Bibliothèque National in Paris, on which this edition is based, contains an alternate violin part which dates from the same period. To avoid an excess of leger lines and clef changes Schubert wrote the arpeggione part almost exclusively in the treble clef which the performer was expected to read an octave lower than written. The work, printed with both violin and cello parts in 1871, was edited for the viola when it came into its own as a solo instrument around the turn of the century. This music remains a standard work in the viola repertoire because its sound qualities and range make it beautifully suited for that instrument.

In this edition the viola part is written as the arpeggione would have sounded, except for a few editorial changes when the original musical line goes below the range of the viola; for comparison and for its historical interest the solo part in the piano score retains Schubert's original arpeggione notation. The editorial additions of dynamics and other performance suggestions appear in the piano score in parentheses, but in the viola part these have been incorporated into the music; brackets in the viola part indicate alternatives.

PAUL DOKTOR

SONATA

(Per Arpeggione)

Viola part
edited and fingered by Paul Doktor

Franz Schubert
(1797-1828)

Allegro moderato

*) The solo line appears here throughout as in Schubert's manuscript, the player being required to play the notes an octave lower than written.

45916cx

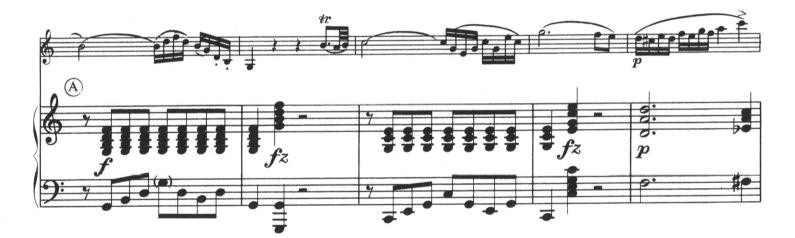

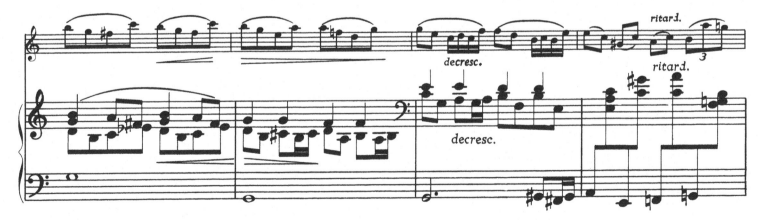

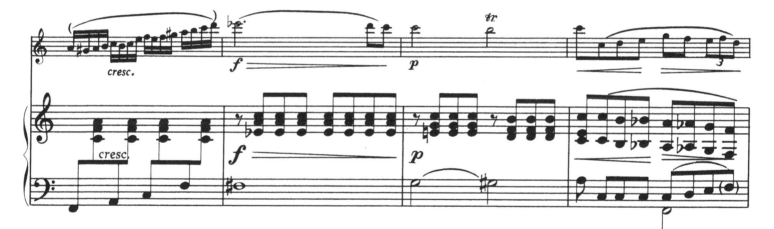

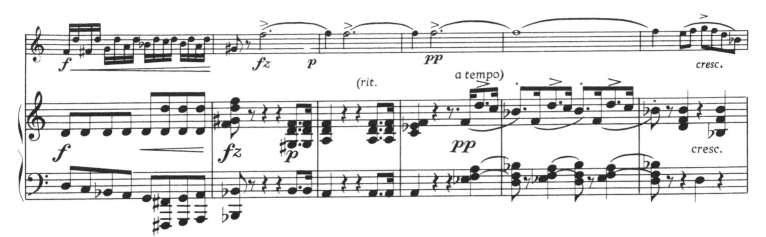

45916

45916

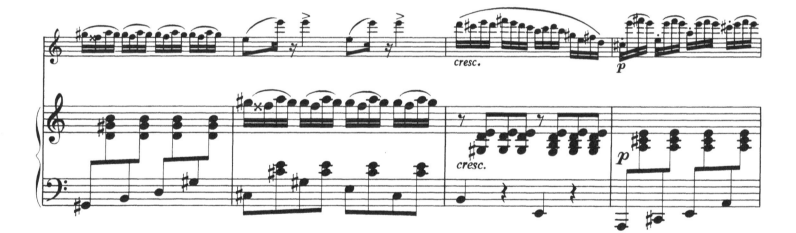

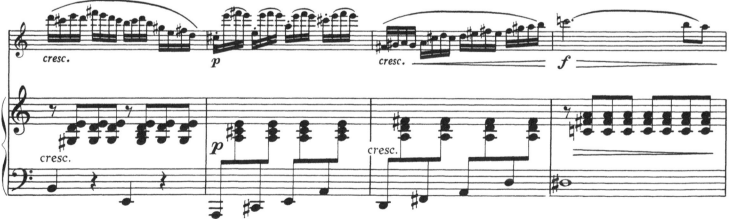

45916

Viola

SCHIRMER'S LIBRARY
OF MUSICAL CLASSICS

Vol. 1832

Franz Schubert

Sonata
(Per Arpeggione)

For Viola and Piano

Viola part edited
and fingered by
PAUL DOKTOR

G. SCHIRMER, Inc.

DISTRIBUTED BY

HAL•LEONARD®
CORPORATION
7777 W. BLUEMOUND RD. P.O. BOX 13819 MILWAUKEE, WI 53213

Photograph of an Arpeggione

Preface

The "Arpeggione" was a guitar-like instrument tuned in the same way as the guitar (E A d g b e′), but held between the knees and played with a bow. Invented in 1821 by the Viennese guitar maker Johann Georg Stauffer (1778-1853), it was originally called "Guitarre d'amour," but soon dubbed "Arpeggione" because it lent itself so well to arpeggio playing. However, its peculiar guitar-like body made adequate performance on it very awkward; especially in loud passages it was very difficult to keep the bow on one string only. But the instrument possessed a warm sound quality, and it was this attribute which Schubert exploited in the sonata which he wrote for it in 1824. Naming his composition *Sonata for Arpeggione,* he honored the instrument's nickname by making it, so to speak, official. However, despite the attention brought to the new instrument through public performances of the Schubert work by Vinzenz Schuster, and the publication of an instruction book by the same musician, the arpeggione soon became obsolete: its beauty of tone could not make up for its playing difficulties and rather small volume of sound.

Schubert's manuscript in the Bibliothèque National in Paris, on which this edition is based, contains an alternate violin part which dates from the same period. To avoid an excess of leger lines and clef changes Schubert wrote the arpeggione part almost exclusively in the treble clef which the performer was expected to read an octave lower than written. The work, printed with both violin and cello parts in 1871, was edited for the viola when it came into its own as a solo instrument around the turn of the century. This music remains a standard work in the viola repertoire because its sound qualities and range make it beautifully suited for that instrument.

In this edition the viola part is written as the arpeggione would have sounded, except for a few editorial changes when the original musical line goes below the range of the viola; for comparison and for its historical interest the solo part in the piano score retains Schubert's original arpeggione notation. The editorial additions of dynamics and other performance suggestions appear in the piano score in parentheses, but in the viola part these have been incorporated into the music; brackets in the viola part indicate alternatives.

PAUL DOKTOR

SONATA

VIOLA

Viola part edited and fingered
by Paul Doktor

Franz Schubert (1797-1828)

Allegro moderato

Adagio

Allegretto

*)

**) upper slurs are in ms.

*) depress "a" silently and hold for two measures
45916 **) m.s. not clear -see also page 9 and footnote in piano part, page 20.

8

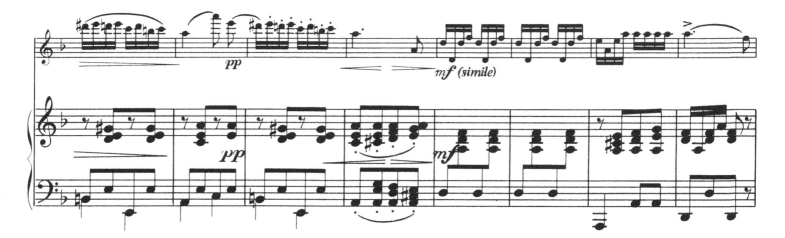

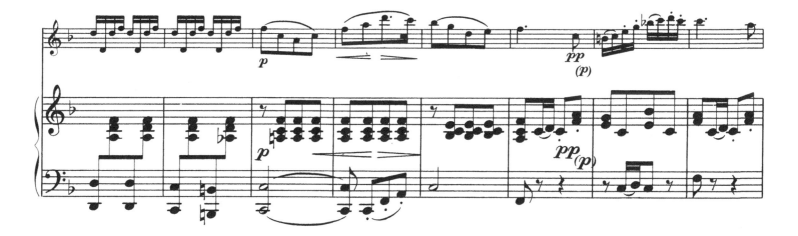

*) Ritardandos and a tempos for this phrase are suggested by the editer because of the inconsistency in the m.s. here and for page 28.

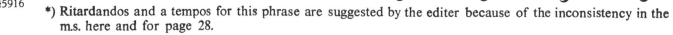

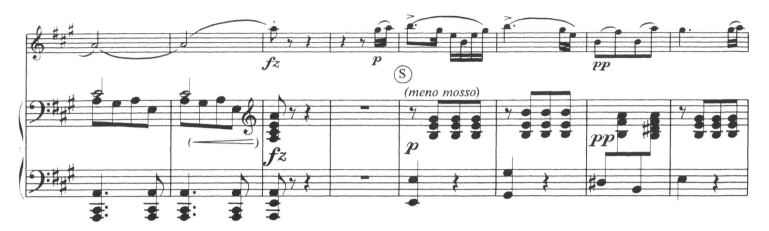

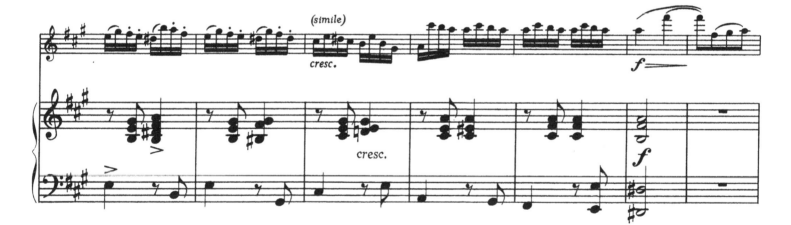

ossia for easier
page turning of
viola part

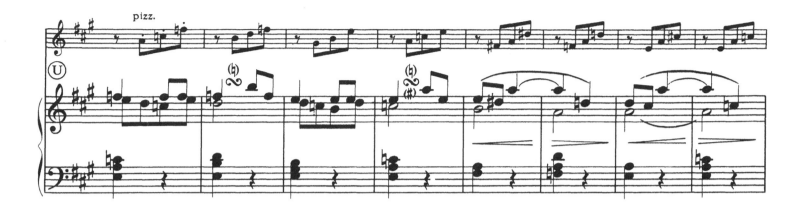

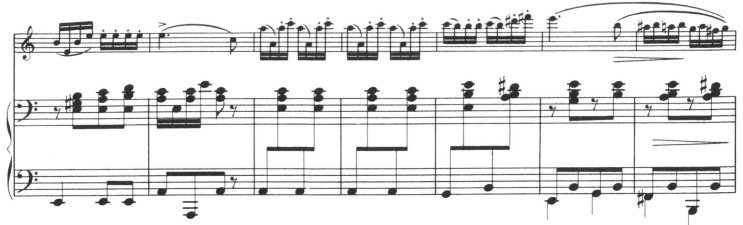

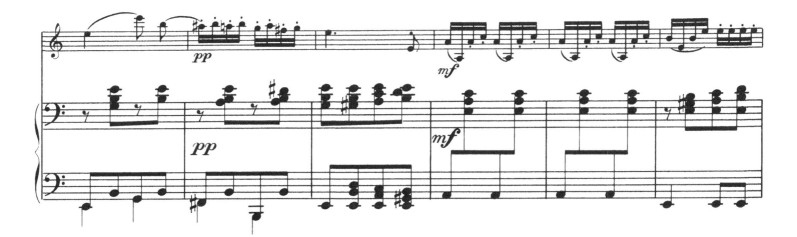

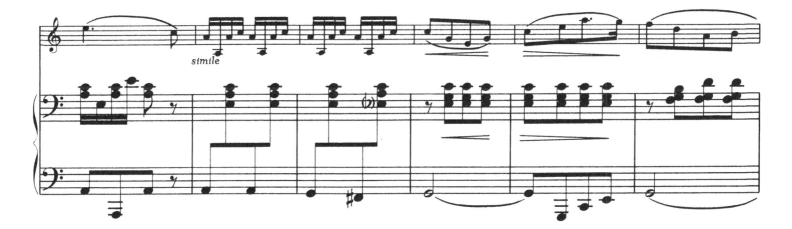

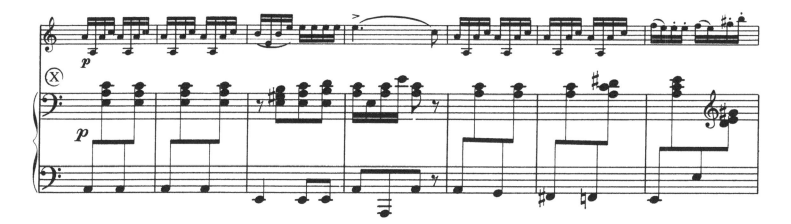

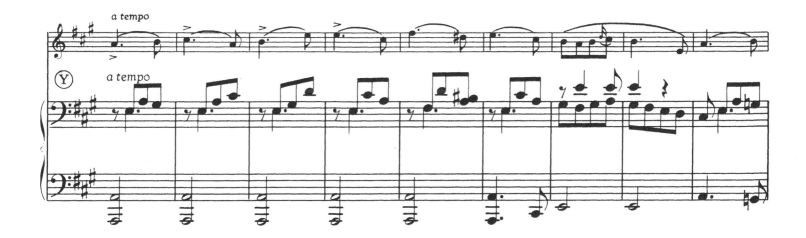

*) See footnote on page 20